HOW TO GET YOURSELF OUT OF JURY DUTY

Jan Miller

Copyright © 2019 Jan Miller

All rights reserved.

ISBN: 9781796235340

DEDICATION

To the hubs, for always keeping me sane.

CONTENTS

Acknowledgments

Introduction   1

Who You Gonna Call?   5

Why Did I Get This?   9

Legal Wriggles   13

Creative Wriggles   53

About the Author   119

For Your Consideration   121

ACKNOWLEDGMENTS

With special thanks to Christina Hamlett
for editorial services
and cover design.

Cover image by Ioulia Bolchakova (123rf)

INTRODUCTION

"Yay! I just got a summons for jury duty!" Said. No One. Ever.

Although one can certainly look at jury service as a civic privilege and opportunity to participate in the American judicial system, the fact of the matter is that most of us believe we really have better things to do with our time.

Getting a root canal.

Watching paint dry.

Standing in line at the Department of Motor Vehicles.

From the moment that ominous envelope arrives in the mail and up until the time we are solemnly herded into a courtroom, our minds are racing with plans to wriggle out of it.

While there are legal disqualifiers for getting dismissed--being a felon, being related to someone in law enforcement, being over the age of 70, being pregnant and dangerously close to popping out a new life--there are also creative excuses, and that's what this book is all about.

My sister, Gwen, for instance, is older than I am but has mastered the knack of donning age-inappropriate ensembles.

Another time she sported an All-Seeing Eye (fake) tattoo on her forehead. These things haven't stopped her from receiving summons, but she has yet to ever advance beyond a short interview in the jury box.

The only two people in my immediate family who were initially excited to get a summons to California Superior Court were our middle daughter (who had just turned 22) and my mother, who had recently relocated here from North Dakota.

Darling daughter had grown up watching reruns of *Perry Mason*, *LA Law*, and *Law and Order* and, thus, perceived that being part of a real-life courtroom tableau could be pretty exciting and heady stuff. It had also not escaped her attention that some of the faux attorneys like Harry Hamlin and Jimmy Smits were good-looking men and, being a single college student, she might snag a new beau who was smart and dressed well. Did I mention she had a drekky part-time job she wasn't keen on and that jury duty—even if it only paid $5 a day—was a respite from tedium?

What she wasn't taking into account is that events move faster on a television program because each week's storyline has to be wrapped up in less than an hour. There are also the unexpected outliers such as Jessica Fletcher from *Murder, She Wrote* who, whilst sitting in the jury box, will suddenly declare, "That's it! Of course! Lemon meringue pie! I *know* who the murderer is!" and politely ask the judge if he might call a recess so she could investigate on her own.

In real courtrooms, these things don't happen. In a nutshell, it is tedium with a capital T.

My mother, in contrast, saw jury duty as an opportunity to sit in a pleasant room all day and catch up on her knitting. She asserts—to anyone who will ask—that knitting is a calming, mindless task which she can perform while watching TV, chatting with friends, listening to music. Had she lived during the French Revolution, she could easily have been Madame Thérèse Defarge (the cackling tricoteuse with a front row seat at the guillotine) who used her craft to stitch faces and names into a woven register of unfortunate decedents. Heads could literally roll by and not distract her in the slightest.

It, thus, came as a rude awakening when prospective jurors were asked to put away anything that might inhibit their full focus on the courtroom proceedings. Cellphones. Laptops. E-readers. Knitting.

Mom was certain she had been singled out, especially since her latest knitting project was in her lap and she was pretty sure no one could even see it. She raised her hand and asked the judge why her knitting was a problem. Taken back a bit by her bold inquiry, he nevertheless explained the importance of having her undivided attention while testimony was being given so that she could help render a fair decision. Mom countered that she could listen and knit at the same time.

"I'm sure you can," the judge replied, "but the thing of it is that I believe it would … " Mom told us that he seemed to scramble for the right phrase to set her straight.

Apparently the best he could come up with was " ... set a precedent for future trials."

Oh, the horror. Vast swaths of knitters flooding the courtroom, their needles clicking away while they cackle maniacally at everything being said.

Suffice it to say, Mom was not only dismissed that day but she also never received a summons thereafter. She is convinced that somewhere in the files there is a mark by her name which labels her as an obstreperous loon.

WHO YOU GONNA CALL?

It has always been my belief that if someone really *wants* to serve on a jury, they should be allowed to. Certainly if *I* were ever on trial for something and was going to have my case judged by a jury of my peers, I would want them to be focused, alert, engaged and genuinely interested in what my attorney and my witnesses had to say.

If my glances toward the jury box revealed 12 people who were (1) struggling to stay awake, (2) constantly checking their watches, (3) fidgeting because they felt they had been taken away from something more important, and/or (4) scrunching their foreheads as if to squeeze cohesive thoughts into their brains, I would not be filled with feelings of unmixed delight.

Over the years, I have tried (without much success) to figure out who's going to be retained and who's going to be dismissed. My daughters gently point out that I'm about as good at this as I am at predicting the winning couples on *Dancing With The Stars*. As dazzled as I may be with the costumes and how artfully the dancers execute a Paso Doble, a sassy Salsa or a seductive Tango, I have never been on the same page with Carrie Ann Inaba, Bruno Tonioli and Len Goodman.

What, exactly, are lawyers really looking for? Individuals that *I* personally think would make perfectly fine candidates are thanked and excused without a blink. Further, they're not offered any explanation or recommendation on how they might perform better next time.

Although it varies from case to case, it's a paradoxical equation in which both sides are looking for individuals who can be impartial and yet sympathetic to their respective clients. The lawyers can't go out and choose/recruit jurors on their own but they *do* have the right to shoo away anyone they believe might harm the interests of whomever they are representing.

Given the random gaggle of personalities set before them, the prosecution and the defense have a short window of time to determine how age, gender, ethnicity, education, occupation, religion and life experiences will make potential jurors more or less receptive to the information they're setting forth about the case.

For instance, how much do you trust authority? Do you believe that doctors, lawyers and police are always correct in the decisions they make or that, being as flawed as anyone else, there's a margin for error in play that necessitates a second or even third opinion? A prosecuting attorney is going to gravitate toward individuals who trust and respect authority. These are people who often harbor the view that if someone is on trial at all, s/he is probably guilty of *something*. In contrast, a defense attorney is seeking out potential jurors who can be open-minded and aren't as likely to just accept everything they hear on the basis of a license, a degree or a badge.

In the days of *Perry Mason*, the only thing sitting on the table in front of either counsel was a legal pad and a pencil in which they could jot down notes about what to ask during cross-examination. Nowadays, both sides have laptops in plain sight and it's a pretty sure bet they're not checking their email or watching cat videos on YouTube. Nope. They're seeing what they can find out about *you*. If you're active on social media, you've left a mighty large footprint for anyone to follow. Have you been outspoken on politics? Do you travel a lot? Are you all about party, party, party? Do you frequently post content related to your religion? If you're prominent in the business community, what causes do you support? What sort of groups, clubs and organizations do you belong to?

Do you project in your clothing and your demeanor a picture of strong and competent leadership? If you do, you're likely to be chosen as the foreperson of the jury and the one to whom 11 other people will look for guidance in rendering a decision. Their collective mindset is, "We really don't want to be here anyway so let's just let the smart person do the thinking *for* us."

This does not escape the attention of the prosecution or the defense. They recognize that a strong leader can influence his/her peers in either direction and, thus, *that's* the person they each need to convince instead of the 11 people sharing the same jury box.

If they anticipate this strong leader won't be on *their* side, they won't want them on the jury. Once you remove a strong leader to herd the group, the group will be left to their own devices to figure things out. If they *can't* figure things out in order to reach a verdict, it becomes a hung (deadlocked) jury, resulting in a mistrial and opening the door for a new trial (and a different jury).

The prosecution won't be terribly happy about this. The defense, however, will be breathing a sigh of relief that a dozen people couldn't come to any accord.

What's on your feet? Bet you didn't know that attorneys are checking out your footwear when you enter the courtroom. Individuals who are nurturing, laid-back and comfortable in their own skin want their footwear to be comfy, too, even if they're going to be sitting all day. This means slip-ons instead of lace-ups, low heels instead of Jimmy Choo stilettos. If your shoes look like they pinch, it's perceived you'll be in a pissy, disagreeable mood and impatient to get this whole thing over with.

I also have to say in all candor that I've never seen anyone picked for a jury who was drop-dead gorgeous (ala Salma Hayek) or dashingly handsome (ala Patrick Dempsey). A lawyer friend told me that it's because anyone who stands out as exceptionally good-looking can potentially be exceptionally *distracting* to everyone else in the courtroom. Both sides prefer jurors who are not only totally average in appearance but even nondescript.

The hubs is certain that this is the very reason he has never been chosen.

WHY DID I GET THIS?

A jury summons is not a Willy Wonka Golden Ticket—a coveted candy wrapper that entitles the bearer to an indulgent visit to a magical candy factory and a lifetime supply of chocolate. There are no rewards for stealing a sample of The Everlasting Gobstopper while you're there, nor is it a morality test to see if you're worthy of having all your dreams come true. If someone walking down the street found a crinkled summons in a rain gutter, s/he wouldn't pounce on it with glee, wave it in the air and say, "I've won! I've won!"

More likely they're too busy trying to figure out how to get rid of the one which arrived in the mailbox with their own name on it.

The rebel response is to throw the U.S. Postal Service under the bus and claim that you never received it. These notices, however, can be tracked electronically. Each state has its own penalties insofar as repercussions for ignoring a civic obligation and they're plainly stated on the summons itself. These range from the imposition of fines to actual warrants for arrest. Yikes! Los Angeles County, by the way, has a reputation for heavily fining people who opt to shirk their civic duty and play hooky.

When roll is called and you're not there, court clerks will follow up by phone or email to find out why. The exception is if they already have more jurors than they need or, frankly, they're just swamped that day and don't get around to it. If you *do* get a call, you probably know that a lot of people resort to the ol' "Oh, my gosh! I must have accidentally thrown it out with the rest of my junk mail." In which case they will simply send you another one.

Busted.

Social media is replete with individuals who brag that they've been tossing out their jury summons for years and nothing has ever happened to them. (Although one has to wonder why they're bragging on a platform that constitutes its own form of paper trail which could come back to bite them.)

There are also those who proudly declare that they are engaging in civil disobedience as a way of protesting the number of frivolous lawsuits by charlatan lawyers taking up everyone's time and that no one can *make* them show up if they don't want to. (Okay, seriously, would you even *want* this rabid level of activism in a case involving minor property damage?)

Let's be honest. At the end of the day, they're going to an awful lot of chancy trouble for a routine event which really isn't that painful to endure. Many states, for example, have adopted a "one day/one trial" system. This means that (1) if you show up on the first day and don't get put on a panel, your jury service for that year is done or (2) if you *are* chosen for a panel, your jury service for the year is complete after that particular trial ends.

For people with day-jobs, this reduces the uncertainty of how long they'll be absent. Unlike earlier years when prospective jurors had to be available every day for two weeks and then for however long *after* that two weeks as was necessary to reach a verdict, participants nowadays are asked to be available for *one* week. Even better, if they're not put on a panel the first day, it cancels out their service for the remainder of that week. Done deal.

If individuals *are* put on a panel, it's not uncommon for the judge to provide an estimate of how long s/he expects the trial to last. While you still have to be available for the full week to which you originally committed, it's reasonable to let the court know if you have any existing obligations *beyond* that week.

If it's something major, of course (i.e., your honeymoon to Cancun), there is an opportunity to request an extension when your jury summons first arrives in the mail rather than waiting until you are actually in the courtroom.

You are eligible for jury duty in your state if:

- You are at least 18 years old.
- You are an American citizen.
- You are capable of understanding English.
- You are not older than 70.
- You have resided in the judicial district for one year.
- You have never been convicted of a felony (unless your civil rights have been legally restored).
- You do not have mental or physical conditions that inhibit your ability to serve.

For federal juries, the following are exempt from service:

- Active members of the Armed Forces.

- Active members of police and fire departments.
- Full-time public officers and elected officials of federal, state and local governments.

Once you're holding that Golden Ticket to peer behind the curtain, what are you going to do with it? We'd like to think that you'll be Charlie Bucket, stride into the factory with a mix of wonder, respect and confidence, and ultimately Do The Right Thing. If you're Augustus Gloop, Veruca Salt, Violet Beauregarde or Mike Teevee, however—well, there's just no saving you from yourself. There are perfectly legal ways to avoid serving. There are creative ways, too, which still fall within the parameters of legitimacy.

Choose wisely.

LEGAL WRIGGLES

The courts get their lists of prospective juror names from voter registration records and from drivers' licenses and ID cards issued by each state's Department of Motor Vehicles. Accordingly, if you've never registered to vote and you've never applied for a driver's license or ID card, you're pretty much living off the grid and beneath the radar and can read the rest of this book purely for its entertainment value.

Depending on the size of the jurisdiction, jury wheels are comprised of hundreds of thousands of names, all of which are randomized. One's placement on those randomized lists accounts for whether s/he gets called every year or never gets called at all. It's also purely coincidence if two people in the same household—a husband and wife, for instance—receive respective summons for the very same week. Nor is it unusual if you have a fairly common last name to hear it multiple times during roll call in the jury waiting room. Luck of the draw.

If you do receive a summons and you meet the criteria in the previous chapter, you'll be expected to show up and do your civic duty. There are, however, a number of perfectly legal exit strategies that will get you off the hook, albeit temporarily.

Many of these can easily be addressed without your ever having to step into the courtroom. For starters, there's a space on the summons form itself in which one can (briefly) describe the inconvenience or hardship that jury service would impose. With more and more jurisdictions now using electronic platforms, this information can be submitted online through a 24/7 web portal.

Antediluvian as it sounds (especially to anyone under the age of 30 who just now had to look up what *antediluvian* even means), there's the option of typing an actual letter and snail-mailing it. This is effective if photocopied attachments (including a copy of the summons) are involved.

Letters—if well written—get attention if for no other reason than so few people take the time to properly write them anymore. A recipient at the court will probably be as gobsmacked as if you had sent in a Willy Wonka Golden Ticket.

Thinking of saving time and just making a phone call? Don't. You'll likely spend as much time waiting on hold as it would have taken to type a letter and put a stamp on it. Even finding a sympathetic listener is no guarantee that s/he will memorialize the conversation or, for that matter, possess the authority to grant any dispensation.

There is, of course, nothing wrong with showing up on the requested date and explaining yourself in person. Visuals can speak volumes. Did you ever, for example, want to take a Friday off at work by feigning a newly caught cold? Calling Friday morning from home is often suspect. Sneezing, coughing and red-rimmed eyes on a Thursday, however, elicits sympathy and generates angst among your coworkers that you're contagious. "Shoo! Shoo! Get out of my face!"

While this latter strategy better fits the chapter on

CREATIVE WRIGGLES, there are nonetheless occasions when seeing (You) truly is believing. Are you more likely to accept the excuse of someone who tells you on the phone that she is pregnant or someone who shows up looking as if she's about to deliver triplets? No brainer.

Okay, so let's take a look at some of the perfectly legal ways to extricate yourself from jury service.

HOW TO GET YOURSELF OUT OF JURY DUTY

"I DON'T LIVE HERE ANYMORE"

If you have physically moved out of the court jurisdiction for which you have been sent a summons, you are no longer eligible to serve on a jury for that locale. You are, however, eligible to serve at your *next* jurisdiction once you have updated your voter registration and driver's license. Bear in mind that moving from a very large county to a significantly smaller one increases your odds of selection, given the number of available bodies to choose from. This, however, should not govern a purposeful choice to move from Loving County (Texas) to Los Angeles.

If you have been away long enough and there's not a forwarding address on file at the post office, the summons will be returned to sender and you'll be none the wiser that it was even mailed to you. If the summons *does* get forwarded to your new abode, all you need do is pop the summons back into the mail with the yellow forwarding label on it and the court will figure out you're no longer available for its jury wheel.

What *doesn't* work is to say, "I've moved!" when all you've done is relocate to a different floor of your current apartment building or across the street (unless that particular street happens to be the dividing line between two separate counties).

Nor can you necessarily get away with declaring, "I'm *planning* to move." Come on now. Everyone's *planning* to do *something*, aren't they? They're *planning* to get married. They're *planning* to have kids. They're *planning* to pay off their debt and move to a remote island in the Bahamas and drink rum. The unspoken word here is *Someday* as opposed to *During the Coincidental Time You Want Me To Serve On A Jury*. The court obviously doesn't have the personnel to come and see if there are packing boxes strewn around your living room. Nor are they likely to inquire, "So where, exactly, are you moving *to*?"

In a nutshell, you could probably get away with this excuse once and never, in fact, move yourself anywhere. Using this as your default, however, will eventually trip you up. Look at how many times the cross-dressing Corporal Klinger from *M*A*S*H* cited ailing, pregnant or deceased relatives as an excuse to push for a Section 8 discharge from Korea. The thick dossier of bogus correspondence kept by Colonels Blake and Potter was frequently brought up as a reminder of ploys that even Klinger himself forgot he had tried.

"THIS ISN'T A GOOD TIME FOR ME"

Is there ever a *good* time to go serve on a jury? Most people would say "no." They have jobs, they have families, they have vacations, they have surgeries, they have weddings and honeymoons. They have a multiplicity of things competing for their time, energy and attention and, suffice it to say, some of these activities simply *can't* be rescheduled in order to accommodate a jury summons.

The courts understand this. Accordingly, there's a mechanism to postpone one's service by requesting an extension. Not every jurisdiction allows this, however. Further, those that *do* grant extensions may require prospective jurors to submit an explanation which will then be reviewed. A request accompanied by a doctor's note, for instance, that the individual requires time to recover from a major medical procedure will be looked upon more favorably than someone who says, "Well, the circus is in town that week and I've really been looking forward to going."

Other jurisdictions are much more liberal in granting extensions online, usually because they don't have the staff to review a plethora of explanations and render wise decisions. In these jurisdictions, you don't have to provide an explanation at all. You can either put off jury service for up to 90 days or provide the court with new dates that you *are* available.

Several things can work in your favor in this regard.

The first is to notify the court as soon as possible if you'd like an extension versus waiting until the Friday before you're supposed to report and saying, "Oh golly, I just remembered the circus is in town next week. Mind if I do that instead?" The more time you give them to figure out how to accommodate your absence, the nicer they will be.

Secondly—and this is if you have an option to get a 90-day extension—take a look at the calendar and see if you'd be better off choosing your *own* range of dates. Let's say that 90 days from now is the middle of January. Whether or not the middle of January is good for you, consider requesting the week before Thanksgiving or the week before Christmas.

Since neither side in a court case warms to the idea of having a trial that could trickle into the holidays, they tend to settle *out* of court or not schedule the trial until the holidays are over. Not your problem. If you're scheduled for jury duty during either of those weeks, the likelihood of your being called is pretty remote. Pre-Easter week, by the by, is another smart choice.

The third option is to request a date that is *earlier* than the (inconvenient) one for which you've been slated. It demonstrates your enthusiasm to serve and will actually confuse the heck out of them. "What? This person wants to come *sooner*?" They'll make note of the fact that you asked but, in most cases, they already *have* the number of jurors they'll be needing. They'll thank you very much and offer to get back to you on that. And then they won't.

OH, BABY!

Pregnant women in their third trimester tend to make strangers nervous (especially men). They are often given a wide berth (no pun intended) so as not to inadvertently jostle the mum-to-be into an early labor.

It's also a fact that pregnant women have frequent occasion to skaddle into restrooms. Courtroom trials are not conducive to sitting for long periods of time on uncomfortable chairs and, further, not being able to nosh on weird snack-craves.

Neither attorney is going to be keen on the idea of an expectant juror. Likewise with the clients they are respectively representing. While not every mum-to-be is going to be stereotypically emotional and/or hormonal, lawyers and judges don't want someone who may have to leave for doctor appointments, midday morning sickness, fatigue or stress.

Even women in their *first* trimester can be excused with a doctor's note if they have had previous miscarriages or their current health foreshadows complications and risks to a successful delivery.

Have you recently given birth to a bouncing bundle of joy? Breastfeeding in a jury box is another distraction to the judicial process. At present, 17 states and Puerto Rico exempt breastfeeding mothers from jury duty or allow jury service to be postponed for up to 12 months. (California, Connecticut, Idaho, Illinois, Iowa, Kansas, Kentucky, Michigan, Mississippi, Missouri, Montana, Nebraska,

Oklahoma, Oregon, South Dakota, Utah and Virginia.)

Jurisdictions vary on whether a doctor's note is required or whether a nursing mum will be taken at her word.

CAREGIVERS

If you are legally and personally responsible for the welfare of a child or children under the age of 16 or you're necessarily responsible for someone with physical or mental impairments which require continuous care and supervision on your part, a doctor's note can get you an excuse from jury duty.

Unfortunately, this is one of the most abused exit strategies that prospective jurors like to use.

For example, everyone knows and accepts that adolescents and teenagers can be a handful. If, however, those offspring are in school during the day and you yourself are holding a full-time job, you don't fit the definition which could qualify you for an exemption.

Likewise if you have a spouse at home who shares in the parenting responsibilities or an au pair you're paying to mind the little tykes while you're away. Clearly they can function without your being there.

Caring for an invalid/incapacitated spouse will get you a pass, as will the care of an elderly relative who permanently *lives* under the same roof with you. A note from a doctor will need to be provided which attests to your legal role as a caregiver. If that role is construed in any way as fuzzy, don't expect it to sway things in your favor. I recall, for instance, a male in the jury waiting room who explained that he was looking after an elderly blind man.

"Is this person a relative of yours?" he was asked.

"Nope."

"Are you being paid for your services as a professional caregiver?"

"Nope, but now and again he gives me money to go buy us beer and chips. Does that count?"

The clerk then asked who was looking after the elderly blind gent while the prospective juror was downtown at the courthouse.

"Nobody," the man said with an indifferent shrug. "But heck, the guy's blind. He can't even find the front door so I don't expect him to go very far if he gets out."

Others have interpreted the caretaker role to encompass house pets that don't like to be left alone all day. Well, who among us animal lovers can blame them for this reasoning? Despite the fact that our pets clearly depend on us for their well-being (even though many of them are content to sleep through the whole day), they can't be offered up as a plausible excuse when it comes to jury duty.

Still, it doesn't stop people from trying.

I recall an elderly lady who came into the jury room with an open-top archive box that contained a rather vociferous duck. (Why she wasn't questioned about this at security is anyone's guess.) "Excuse me, ma'am," a clerk finally spoke up, "but why did you bring a duck?"

Without missing a beat, the woman replied, "Well, I can't leave him at home. He just gets into things."

FINANCIAL HARDSHIP

Restaurant servers don't like getting jury summons. If they don't work, they don't get paid. Conversely, civil servants don't mind jury summons at all, especially if they don't really like their jobs and/or their bosses. In the government sector, their employers are required by law to release them for jury service. They still get paid as if they were physically at the office, and the only requirement is to surrender any pittance fees they receive if they actually get put on a panel for x number of days.

Lunch breaks for jurors are often 90 minutes, which is 30-45 minutes more than what they usually get on their day job. Coupled with the amount of time one spends sitting around in the waiting room reading novels and checking emails, what's *not* to like about it? It's like a lackadaisical detention hall without any homework or glaring teachers.

If your employer believes your presence at work is extremely critical to the life's blood of the organization (and why is this value never articulated in annual performance reviews?), it is incumbent upon him or her to write a letter to the court and request an exemption *for* you. On the one hand, it gets you off the hook for having to come up with a cunning excuse on your own. ("Seriously, Your Honor. I really *wanted* to be there and do my part but my boss said no. Go figure."

Think of it as saying, "I really wanted to go to the concert but Mom says I'm grounded.")

On the other hand, a 90-minute lunch at someplace other than the office cafeteria would have been nice …

So what happens if an individual is a sole proprietor or the only person in a business, commercial or agricultural enterprise who is qualified to perform an essential task? Specifically, if the services performed are crucial to the livelihood of the business and said business would be forced to cease operation for whatever amount of time the juror is away, there is sufficient cause to request an exemption. An individual who provides childcare during the week for others, for instance, has a fairly clear-cut case because of the ripple-effect an inconvenient jury service could create for the working families who are depending on her services.

The summons form will contain information on how to claim financial hardship. This may include the provision of a written letter and supporting materials such as recent bank statements. In the case of sole proprietors, details will be required to substantiate why the services being provided would be in dire jeopardy if everything had to be put on hold.

Suffice it to say, writers, artists and musicians—many of them solopreneurs—don't fit this category despite the unabashed passion they pour into their projects and the belief that the world is breathlessly waiting for their next creation.

The world, alas, may need to wait a smidge longer.

STUDENT BODIES

Students who are of legal age are not exempt from being jurors.

Okay but seriously, would you really *want* students serving on the jury if you were the plaintiff or the defendant? Students have way too many things going on in their heads to focus and make informed decisions regarding guilt and innocence.

Among these are weighty matters such as:

- Why hasn't my hangover from last night's kegger gone away yet?
- When is the next kegger?
- Where is the next kegger?
- Should I switch my major again?
- Where did I leave my homework?
- Did I even *do* my homework?
- How am I going to pay off my student loans?
- Where will I live if my parentals kick me out of the basement?
- Where should I go on Spring break?
- Where can I *afford* to go on Spring break?
- Does So-and-So like me?
- Does So-and-So really, *really* like me?
- Should I have taken a gap year?
- Has my ex started seeing anyone?

- Can I get my ex back?
- Has my ex been talking about me?
- Why can't my roommates pick up after themselves?
- What do I watch after *Game of Thrones* is all over?
- Could I seriously date someone who has never seen a single episode?
- Why is my period late?
- Why is my girlfriend pushing to get married?
- When do we get to go to lunch?
- Should I become vegan?
- Is there life on other planets?
- Why are these chairs so uncomfortable?

Don't get me wrong. I adore students. I've even known a number of them (my own daughters and their friends included) who *could* pay attention and take the role of being a jurist seriously.

At the end of the day, though, I put this in the same category as those who want to lower the voting age to 16 and the driving age to 14. Both are much too young to make smart (and safe) choices that will affect others.

So let's now say you're a student who *wants* to get out of jury duty.

Are you attending school full-time? It doesn't qualify as an excuse, but many states will allow you to postpone your service until school isn't in session. To accommodate this request, some courts will ask you to produce a student ID and proof of your status as a full-time enrollee. (Obviously this excuse will not work if the summons arrives during the summer months if/when you're kicking back on summer break and not taking any classes.)

Deferrals are typically allowed for full-time students only, not part-time. Nor do deferrals apply to students taking online classes, continuing and community education extension courses, or night schools.

Important exams or presentations coming up that you can't afford to miss? The courts may ask you to provide the dates of your school terms and semester breaks as well as a written schedule of exams from your instructors. This, however, is no guarantee of a deferral to a more convenient time.

If you live in a jurisdiction that *isn't* going to grant a deferral, the first step is to provide the Dean's office with written verification of the call to jury duty. If the service is short-term (i.e., five days or less), your instructors will be advised to make arrangements to accommodate the exams and assignments you'll have to miss.

If it's going to be for longer than five days, the Dean's office can make arrangements to ensure your academic work gets completed. In the event you have to withdraw from all or part of the class, this will be without penalty. Further, you can request a full refund of the tuition and associated fees for the credit hours you were not able to complete.

So what happens if you attend school out-of-state but you still identify your parents' house as your home address? In most cases, you'll be considered a resident of the state where you were living before you left for school and not a resident of the state where your school is physically located. Your name may, thus, have been drawn based on the perception that your permanent address is the one you're currently not living in. The status quo changes, however, if you take out a driver's license, have employment or live in an apartment within the same jurisdiction as the place you attend classes.

"I THINK I KNOW THIS GUY"

A former neighbor of ours is one of those people who seems to get called for jury duty every single year. And every single year—just like clockwork—he always gets dismissed. The reason is that he always recognizes at least one person in the courtroom as someone he personally knows.

This obviously isn't to say that he runs with a felonious crowd whose members keep showing up on trial. No, he's just a really gregarious guy who works in sales, frequents the most popular eateries and schmoozes at Chamber of Commerce mixers, Toastmasters and Kiwanis.

Plus the fact I can't begin to tell you how many photocopiers and other office equipment he sells to law firms, insurance companies and hospitals—a gig that allows him to regularly cross paths with lawyers, insurance agents and medical professionals.

Yep. Exactly the contingent that argues cases for their clients or gets called upon to offer expert testimony. On one occasion, he even knew the presiding judge as someone he used to play golf with.

It doesn't stop there, either. He can often be found chatting it up in the jury room with friends, neighbors, former coworkers. Even when he's chatting it up with a total stranger, there's such a display of conviviality and easy camaraderie which manages to trigger the Spidey Senses of lawyers as a potential red flag. Could this chatty guy be an influencer of verdict outcomes?

Best, perhaps, to choose someone else.

Prior to panel members being officially selected, there's going to be a question along the lines of, "Do you know the Plaintiff? The Defendant? Either of the counsel? Anyone else in this courtroom?"

For the record: "I think maybe I've seen that guy shopping at Trader Joe's" is obviously not as substantive a reply as "So-and-so used to work for me." Intimate and specific knowledge of an individual and his/her activities and personality carries a certain level of bias. You're supposed to be fair and impartial, right?

My sister Gwen takes the intimacy definition a step deeper. If either of the attorneys is male, attractive and close to her own age, she'll feign a perplexed stare, scrunch her forehead as if she's thinking a really serious thought, and then ask, "Didn't you and I used to have a thing back in college?"

Talk about instantly titillating a courtroom. Especially since Gwen isn't exactly the kind of girl one takes home to meet Mum. In a nutshell, she's a Ginger, not a Mary Ann.

Following the attorney's bewildered flummox, she sweetly apologizes for the mistake and tells him, "Well, like they say, everybody's got a twin …"

BEEN THERE, DONE THAT

If you live in a jurisdiction that follows the One & Done rule, you can't be called for jury duty more than once a year. In the olden days if a person was summoned for jury duty, s/he was expected to show up at the courthouse every single day for two weeks. If they weren't put on a panel during that stretch, their service was considered complete.

Nowadays, prospective jurors only have to show up for *one* day unless they are assigned to a courtroom and subsequently selected for a trial. If they're *not* chosen after a day at the courthouse, they are thanked for their time and sent home with a slip of paper which attests to their service being done for the next 12 months.

Word to the wise: Hang on to that slip of paper if you need to prove that you are being summoned back prematurely.

Speaking of premature actions, if the clock is nudging toward 4-ish and you haven't as yet been assigned a courtroom, never assume that you are free and clear to just get up and leave. If you leave before you get the greenlight to do so, you won't get that slip of paper.

Oh and by the way, you don't get *paid* for that one day of sitting around.

HOW TO GET YOURSELF OUT OF JURY DUTY

WELL, TO BE TOTALLY HONEST …

When you're assigned to a courtroom, you'll either find yourself on a panel for a civil case or a criminal case.

Know the difference?

A civil case is usually a dispute wherein an individual or an entity sues another individual or entity for failing to deliver on a legal obligation or for what they believe to be infringement of their constitutional rights.

In a nutshell, someone in a civil case believes they have been done wrong and they have come to court to collect damages from the wrongdoer.

Examples:

- Breach of contract
- Child custody disputes
- Property damage
- Defamation of character
- Personal injury

A criminal case is all about serious, felonious charges such as murder, kidnapping, embezzlement, etc. Criminal cases involve actions and behaviors that are considered to be harmful to society. Federal crimes are prosecuted by the United States Attorney General's Office whereas as state crimes are prosecuted by the state's Attorney General or a local District Attorney. Only the government can initiate prosecution in criminal cases.

Examples:

- Homicide
- Rape
- Assault
- Drug possession and sale
- Obstruction of justice
- Arson

Another major difference between these two types of courtroom trials revolves around the word "intent."

Civil cases are often about negligence and/or ignorance. Accidentally causing a collision because you were going over the posted speed limit or causing someone to slip on your walkway because you were too lazy to shovel the snow constitutes a failure to follow city codes and rules.

You didn't hit that other car intentionally, nor were you giggling behind a curtain when you saw someone approaching your house and about to take a nasty tumble. In all likelihood, you didn't think there'd be any consequences because, frankly, you were just being distracted or stupid.

In contrast, purposely killing someone, setting fire to a forest or engaging in activities for the purpose of defrauding unwitting victims means that you stayed up nights figuring out how to put your cunning plan into play. In other words, *intentionally* breaking the law just because you thought you were smart enough to get away with it.

Whether you get called for a civil or a criminal panel, you're going to be asked whether you yourself have ever been a victim of a crime. In a civil court, there will be asked for a show of hands. This is then followed by an inquiry as to what *type* of crime was involved. In making their jury selections, the attorneys for both sides use this as a way to gauge whether prospective participants will be sensitive to the charges brought against their clients. Someone whose house was vandalized, for instance, is not going to have much sympathy for an alleged vandal on trial.

In criminal cases, prospective jurors fill out a questionnaire in advance which asks questions such as whether they are familiar with the case at hand from watching media coverage, talking about it with family and friends, etc. With a high-profile murder case, for example, you would have to have been living at the bottom of a well not to have heard anything and, accordingly, started to fashion your own conclusions about guilt or innocence.

Unlike oral questioning as a group (where individuals are not likely to be as honest for fear of being judged if they give a "socially unpopular" reply), the private questionnaire is allowed to go deeper insofar as asking questions which jurors would not feel comfortable answering aloud in front of others. The purpose of these questions is to identify actual bias vs. implied bias.

Actual bias is when an individual candidly admits that s/he could not render a fair and impartial decision based on their personal biases and beliefs.

Implied bias is when an individual's personality traits and life experiences have created a predisposition in favor of one party over the other, regardless of him/her *saying* they could be fair and impartial.

If in your heart of hearts you honestly feel you cannot be objective about a case (i.e., "my experience with [fill in the blank] has always been negative"), you will not be penalized for it if you respectfully admit your bias upfront. The attorneys and their clients would much rather see you dismissed rather than put you through an ordeal which would (1) cause you to revisit unpleasant experiences from the past or (2) compel you to base your decision on a first impression ("I really don't like that guy's weird hair") which may not be valid or relevant to the case.

IN 'N' OUT PATIENTS

If you have an upcoming surgery, no one expects you to add to your emotional and physical stress by having to sit on a jury. Missing medical appointments and treatments or having to postpone a critical procedure could jeopardize your health, and the courts know this.

Likewise, an individual who has just undergone back surgery, a mastectomy or liposuction isn't going to be up and about in short order and ready to hang around in a jury box all day.

The courts are also sensitive to the fact that everyone has different thresholds of pain and bounce-back-iness. Someone in healthy condition who has just had prostate surgery, for instance, could conceivably be back in the office within three days while someone who has had a cosmetic procedure on their eyelids might need to recuperate for several weeks.

The courts base their decisions on what the doctors themselves have to say (in *written* documentation) since they presumably know their patients best.

HOW TO GET YOURSELF OUT OF JURY DUTY

ANIMAL ASSISTED THERAPY

The notion that animals can assist in the emotional well-being of humans has been around since the 18th century. Early asylums in England made the discovery that having small, domesticated animals on the grounds not only served to calm the patients but contributed to higher morale and socialization as well.

Following World War I, the U.S. military began introducing dogs as a comforting, rehabilitative approach to psychiatric patients, especially those whose severe trauma from wartime experiences and injuries inhibited their ability to communicate. Around the same time, dogs were also introduced as "pet therapists" to young children who were emotionally unstable or withdrawn.

Nowadays, assistance animals are used for a wide range of disabilities including vision and hearing impairments, mobility assistance for individuals with muscular dystrophy, spinal cord injuries and arthritis, seizure alert and response, diabetic alerts, autism support and allergy detection.

Service animals are also used for conditions which might otherwise seem "invisible" to other humans including anxiety, depression, agoraphobia, bipolar disorders and fears stemming from post-traumatic stress disorder.

What does this have to do with jury service?

In the first place, you can't be denied entrance to the courtroom (or anywhere else, for that matter) if your service or emotional support dog has been deemed therapeutic to your health and emotional stability. Such animals are protected under the Fair Housing Amendments Act and the Air Carrier Access Act if the animal's owner meets the criteria entitling him or her to such assistance. Did I mention that these animals need to be registered and wear identifying vests and tags?

(For more information on the requirements, visit (https://www.officialservicedogregistry.com/register-your-dog/register-your-emotional-support-dog/).

That said, however, not everyone feels comfortable being around dogs (of *any* size or breed), and your fellow jurors may fit that category. Whether the aversion is cultural, stems from scary experiences with dogs as a child or adult, or relates to allergies or asthma, it could be cause for either dismissing you (and your pooch) or dismissing the person who says, "Eeeeek! There's a strange dog sitting next to me!"

My bet is that the court will excuse you and your dog even if the latter is the best behaved canine on the planet. That's okay. Your dog would have been bored anyway and would much rather spend the day at the park.

RUN THAT BY ME ONE MORE TIME

If you are currently in training for a marathon or, even better, in training on the U.S. Olympic team, you can likely request a postponement of jury service. A friend of my husband's was on the U.S. Yachting team, a commitment which required her to take a leave of absence from work for an entire year. By the time she returned, the court had pretty much forgotten about her.

If you're training for a marathon that coincides with jury duty, your chances of getting a postponement are better if it's (1) a really rigorous marathon and (2) a marathon that people have actually heard of (i.e., the Boston Marathon, the Los Angeles Marathon, the Big Sur International, the NYC Marathon, the Bay to Breakers, etc.).

If it's just a fun run to raise money for your child's school but only covers a distance of 2K (1.24 miles), don't expect much sympathy from a judge.

IT GOES AGAINST MY FAITH

During the Vietnam War, scores of young men fled to Canada in order to avoid being drafted. Whether or not they actually belonged to a recognized religion, the label "conscientious objector" was ascribed to anyone who believed on the basis of moral grounds that he could not discharge weapons, blow things up or in any way, shape or form take the lives of other people within the framework of military combat.

For those who didn't flee northward, the options were to be conscripted anyway but assigned jobs in non-combat units, accepting civilian service in lieu of conscription, participating in protest marches, enduring public censure, and even going to jail as punishment for not wanting to serve.

The United States was neither the only country nor the first to deal with the challenges of pacifist mindsets during times of war. It should also be pointed out that other countries have not been nearly as lenient historically in making accommodation. Among their remedies: detention, forced recruitment, court-martial, imprisonment and execution.

For jury selection in criminal cases—especially those which carry sentences of life imprisonment or the death penalty—prospective jurors will always be asked whether their religious beliefs are potentially incompatible with the duties associated with serving on a case; i.e., sitting in judgment of someone else's behavior and actions. Although it should be noted that many jurisdictions do *not* provide an excuse from jury duty on the basis of religious or moral beliefs, it is still mandatory to show up at the courthouse on the day of the summons. Once there, you can make your argument and will likely be dismissed.

And just in case you wondered, clergymen are *not* exempt from jury duty. By virtue of their busy profession, however, they are theoretically "on call" for their flocks 24/7 and, accordingly, could be subject to too many interruptions over the course of a trial. Can you imagine G. K. Chesterton's *Father Brown* sitting on a jury and Mrs. McCarthy bustling in every half hour to tell him there's been another murder in Kembleford …

The issue of moral and religious objections to jury service in a civil case doesn't carry nearly the weight of that involved in criminal proceedings. While one might assert that "Only God can make a tree," a mere mortal is probably capable of deciding whether the person who cut down that tree in his neighbor's front yard should have to make reparations.

CAN'T GET THERE FROM HERE

One of the reasons that courthouses are built in places which can easily be accessed by foot, car or public transportation is that it eliminates the excuse of, "Sorry, I have no way of getting there."

And yet people still try it anyway.

If, for example, the individual doesn't own a car, the court will likely ask, (1) Can you take a bus or train, (2) Do you have a friend or relative who can drive you, (3) Why not call a taxi, Uber or Lyft?

For the second and third questions, an individual's response might be that s/he doesn't *have* any friends, isn't on speaking terms with her/his relatives, doesn't want to inconvenience anyone, or simply can't afford the expense of a ride service. It could also be that the individual *does* have a car but has so many DUIs s/he isn't allowed to drive it.

Well, okay, you kinda have to feel sorry for people who have absolutely no relationships they can count on. You also can't really ding them for not being able to pay a total stranger to ferry them back and forth, especially if they end up getting put on a panel for a trial that lasts several days. It's, therefore, the court's discretion to decide where the individual is being honest and truly has a transportation problem.

The bus or train issue is one that can easily enough be looked up. The court, in fact, may assume that you already went online and figured out the logistics yourself. They *may* (and the operative word is "may") be amenable to letting you off the hook if you live in a rural area not serviced by public transportation or if it would take multiple transfers—and, thus, an excessive amount of time—just to *get* from your home to the courthouse. All it takes is one missed connection en route and you run the risk of being late. Nobody likes a tardy juror who holds up the proceedings.

The court will also take into consideration whether there is another courthouse within the same county and jurisdiction which is actually closer. In a bit of irony, a good friend of mine lives within easy walking distance of the courthouse in Pasadena and yet always gets a summons for the courthouse which is located in downtown Los Angeles. It's only a distance of 12 miles driving a car but—well, you've heard about LA traffic, haven't you? Especially during rush hour?

Go figure.

STRAIGHT ON TIL MOURNING

During the Victorian era, a death in the family required the survivors to observe a strict code of propriety. If a widow, for instance, failed to grieve on a grand scale and absent herself from society (and particularly non-relative male acquaintance) for at least two years and sometimes even four, she may as well not return to the land of the living at all. Children were expected to mourn for 12 months following the loss of a parent. No playing. No bright clothes. No laughing out loud. Siblings and grandparents were accorded variable periods of weepy respect depending on the degree of affection and adjacency.

Given the century's dark mortality rate and plethora of infectious diseases, death was a frequent caller on both sides of the Atlantic. There was even a thriving business in the 1870s of "death kits" for children's dolls so that their young owners could accustom themselves at an early age to picking out funeral outfits and tucking their toys into little coffins. Household clocks were stopped at the time of death as a perpetual reminder of one's loss. Mirrors and furniture were covered. Anyone who crossed the threshold of a deceased's home—including dogs, cats and chickens—were required to wear black ribbons to keep death from spreading to the outside world.

Adjusting to a "new normal" embraces a multiplicity of

factors including age, gender, culture, religion and whether the death was sudden and unexpected (i.e., an accident) or was a long time in coming. Even in this modern day and age, there is no one-size-fits-all insofar as what constitutes a suitable amount of time for grieving. When it comes to employers, there is an expectation that 3-5 days off (with or without pay) is sufficient for making arrangements, settling family affairs and attending a funeral or memorial service.

How well an individual will be able to perform job duties and other responsibilities *following* his/her return, however, is another matter entirely. If the employee is too deeply in sorrow to successfully function, it's at the discretion of the employer to extend the bereavement leave.

So what do you do if the loss occurs during the time you're called for jury duty?

Jury summons are typically sent out far in advance so recipients can plan their lives around it. Obviously you can't say, "No, six weeks from now really doesn't work because I think there's going to be a death in the family." (This sort of declaration would either suggest you are psychic or you are planning to play an instrumental part in the exit.) If that death occurs shortly *before* or *during* the time you've been put on a panel, you can be excused if the deceased is:

- Your spouse or domestic partner
- Your offspring
- Your parents

- Your siblings
- Your grandparents
- Your in-laws
- A relative who resides in your home

(Savvy readers will note that the staggering demise of a favorite fictional character on, say, *Game of Thrones*, does not constitute a "death in the family." This, however, clearly did not stop squillions of Americans from calling in sick the Monday after *GoT*'s finale because they could not cope with the end of such an addictively epic series.)

Meanwhile, back in reality ...

Although you may or may not be required to provide proof to the court in the form of a death certificate or obituary notice, there is no way for the court to gauge your true degree of inconsolability. A floodgate of crocodile tears, for instance, could actually be masking secret glee and unmixed delight that a demanding parent has finally bitten the dust. Conversely, a "brave face" may be the product of years of conditioning not to show emotion, no matter how devastated one feels on the inside.

Surprisingly enough, courts have also been known to be empathetic to other types of grieving such as the loss of a beloved pet, the break-up of a marriage or engagement, the deployment of a loved one to a combat zone, etc. If your focus is going to be on anything other than being in the courtroom, it's better for everyone all around if your service can be postponed to a later time.

Word of caution: Don't play the sympathy card if it's not, in fact, true. Karma has a way of dealing with duplicity.

CREATIVE WRIGGLES

When I first told friends I was writing this book, there were several who asked if I didn't feel a teensy bit guilty for encouraging people to avoid what is a civic responsibility. Not all countries, they pointed out, have jury systems in place and, accordingly, a person's fate (including life itself) rests entirely in the hands of a judge who brings his/her personal bias into the equation.

Wouldn't it be a *privilege* to be part of a longstanding tradition which ensures justice has been served?

Most definitely … except that not everyone has the patience, sensibility, empathy, intelligence, attention span, integrity, self-awareness, courage and discipline to make informed decisions within the context of a courtroom "team."

In a perfect world, every juror would possess these attributes.

For example, if I were ever charged with anything that required me to seek legal counsel and have a case put together, these are the kind of people I'd want on the panel.

If, however, I thought for a nanosecond that any of them believed they were there under duress and just wanted it done with as fast as possible so they could go to the circus—well, you get the picture. People who don't want to be somewhere are more likely to make hasty decisions than those who have graciously heeded the call and are prepared to buckle down and get serious.

The prior section dealt with perfectly legitimate (and legal) excuses for dismissal. If having gone through it and discovered nary an excuse that fits your *own* circumstances, sometimes you have no choice but to be creative.

Most importantly, none of the following ideas will put you in contempt for disobedience, disruption or being disrespectful of any officers of the court, the attorneys, the clients or your fellow jurors.

Subtlety is the secret to carrying off even the most outrageous charade or kooky persona. The more naturally you can do this and successfully project "Yeah, this is how I look, act and comport myself all the time," the more likely you'll be perceived as the *last* person in the room to whom critical decisions could be entrusted.

Or ... you can just enjoy these whimsical excuses for their priceless entertainment value. Courthouses always encourage prospective jurors to bring along a book to read whilst waiting to hear if they'll be selected. Taking *this* book might have the added benefit of getting you noticed.

HOW TO GET YOURSELF OUT OF JURY DUTY

FRIDA'S UNIBROW

Who knew that your own eyebrows could be an asset in getting you dismissed from jury duty? Let's face it. When you meet someone new and the very first thing you notice about them is the hair above their eyes, it quickly becomes impossible to look anywhere else on their face.

Those facial hairs—intentionally or otherwise—communicate volumes about the owners' personalities and emotions.

For instance:

- Frida Kahlo and *Sesame Street*'s Bert sport the same black unibrow and project artsy and rugged individualism that should not be crossed or contested. I'd put *Angry Bird* into the same mix with his signature black "V" between his eyes. Even if he were happy, he'd still look peeved and not one to be messed with.

- Marilyn Monroe's brows were perfectly sculpted, pointed arches that conveyed bright-eyed innocence and a state of perpetual surprise. Contrast this same design to *Maleficent* (both the animated version and

Angelina Jolie) where the brow bone is shaded with intense blue and purple to match her sinister mood.

- Regular arches that are neither too thick, too thin, too high nor too low are like Baby Bear's porridge: just right. They are drama-free and straightforward. Thus, they project that the person wearing them will be pretty easy to get along with.

- Joan Crawford favored high, thick arches that made her look menacing, masculine and especially haughty when one was lifted independently of the other. It might be something you want to practice in front of a mirror if you want to come across as skeptical and questioning.

- Grace Slick and Mr. Spock? Both keen on half the brow line being erased and the other half sweeping upward in otherworldly cynicism.

- Do bleached brows make a creepy statement? Rooney Mara seemed to think so in *The Girl With The Dragon Tattoo*.

- Shaving one's eyebrows off completely and drawing in new ones with a Sharpie has been popular with pop stars, a throwback to when Marlene Dietrich and Greto Garbo used eyebrow pencils to create a deceptively fragile, ultra-thin look.
- And let's not forget, Groucho Marc, Andy Rooney and John L. Lewis—all of whom had ginormous, fuzzy, messy eyebrows worthy of their own zip codes.

What all of this means to you as a prospective juror is that if your eyebrows are upstaging the rest of you, they will be a distraction to everyone else in the room. If they have been expertly tweezed, microbladed, tinted and maintained, it speaks to the individual's obsessions with perfection. S/he might have a hard time making decisions because those decisions have to absolutely reflect the best possible choice. If they have been left to grow out haphazardly every which way, personal grooming takes a backseat to being an *au natural* free spirit.

Perhaps paying attention isn't a high priority, either.

HOW TO GET YOURSELF OUT OF JURY DUTY

NOT A LOOK FOR EVERYONE

What to wear, what to wear …

A courtroom is a professional setting and, accordingly, the courts expect prospective jurors to dress appropriately as a show of respect. Unfortunately, there are a whole lot of people who don't even dress appropriately for the jobs they go to every day.

Once upon a time there were rules called dress codes, and employers were within legal rights to send someone home to change if they were in violation of those rules. I personally trace the decline of smart office dress to the Dot.Com heyday of the 1990s when employers began taking a page from Hawaii's "Aloha Fridays" and allowing staff to get an early jump on the weekend with jeans, casual shirts, sneakers and leaving ties and jackets at home.

Before they realized it, "Casual Friday" became indistinguishable from the rest of the week. In the 21st century, dress codes have relaxed even more with the advent of employee rights groups saying that criticism of one's appearance infringes on his/her freedom of expression and individuality and can now be construed as harassment.

At least the courts are a last hold-out in insisting that individuals need to dress the part if they're to participate in something as serious as legal proceedings. On the court's website, you'll find a specific set of instructions on what constitutes "appropriate" dress. Among these:

- No shorts.
- No see-through or provocative clothing.
- No flip-flops, sandals or bedroom slippers.
- No tee-shirts with offensive images or slogans.
- No undershirts or tank tops worn by themselves.
- No caps, hats or hoodies.
- No clothing that bares the back, chest or midriff.
- No sagging or low-riding pants.
- No excessively short mini-skirts.
- No strapless dresses.
- No spiked accessories.
- No political campaign buttons.
- No masks or costumes.

- No clothing intentionally torn in inappropriate or suggestive places.
- No bathing suits. (Yes, you have to suspect someone must have tested this to have it made an official rule.)

These things (one would think) should all be common sense. Lawyers used to advise that jurors should dress as if they were going to a job interview.

Except until it became obvious that many of them—especially the 20s crowd—didn't know how to dress for a job interview, either.

If you purposely break any of the dress code rules, you can expect to summarily be sent home to change. They will also expect you to *return* to the courthouse without dawdling and not just go wandering off.

Within these dress code rules, however, there's a lot of latitude to slyly distinguish yourself as someone who should be thanked and excused. Here are some of our favorites.

SUITED FOR SUCCESS

Whether you're a man or a woman, wearing a smartly tailored

business suit (black, navy or dark grey), a starched shirt, polished shoes and (if you're a guy) a power tie and silk pocket square will inevitably have everyone around you think that you're an attorney. Dollars to doughnuts, you'll probably be dressed *better* than the lawyers themselves. This will only serve to intimidate them and make them perceive you as a savvy and stylish distraction to their own spin in the judicial spotlight.

You will also be better dressed than your peers, many of whom tend to dress as if they (1) just came in from doing gardening or (2) dressed in the dark and threw on whatever wasn't in the clothes hamper. (Golly, but can you really help it if you're such an unapologetic fashion plate?) Can you imagine if *everyone* in the courtroom dressed impeccably well? Spectators would wonder if they had stumbled onto the set of *Perry Mason*.

STARS AND STRIPES FOREVER

You obviously can't drape yourself in an American flag when you show up for jury duty but wearing a navy skirt, a white blouse and a flowing red scarf certainly shouts "patriot," doesn't it?

Purple has long been associated with nobility, power … and

snooty impatience.

On the flip side, orange (many people's least favorite color) conjures thoughts of prison jumpsuits. The popularity of *Orange Is The New Black* has only reinforced this.

Khaki and olive combinations subliminally suggest that the park or forestry service is operating with one ranger short.

In a similar vein, my middle daughter once had a really cute belted dress that consisted of a black and white striped, short-sleeved top and black culottes.

My husband always teased her that all she needed was a whistle around her neck and she could go out on a field and referee a game. I'm sure that imagery wouldn't be lost in a courtroom, either.

WHAT SEASON IS THIS?

I don't know about you but whenever I see someone wearing a heavy sweater in the middle of summer or a gauzy cotton dress in winter when, by all accounts, they should be freezing, it makes me feel uncomfortable.

Do they have circulatory problems that might interfere with their judgment? Or have they just not looked at a calendar lately?

HOW TO GET YOURSELF OUT OF JURY DUTY

The only drawback to this approach is that you might get picked as a juror anyway and then have to swelter or shiver your way through the whole trial.

MY BEST LOOK EVER (NOT)

Not everyone has stellar fashion sense. They choose colors, fabrics and styles that simply don't flatter their shapes and complexions and yet go out the front door thinking they really look awesome. They'll button up polyester suit coats that look a size too small, wear trousers that are too short, pair horizontal striped skirts with floral blouses, don nubby leg warmers that (with the exception of ballerinas) haven't been in vogue since the 70s, flaunt fussy frills and flounces that widen one's existing girth, fixate on Peter Pan collars, bright polka dots, velour jumpsuits, granny-square vests, epaulets, *Dynasty* shoulder pads and wild jungle prints, or any other clothing which looks as if it were borrowed from the closet of a younger sibling or an older relative.

Poor things. What were they thinking? Or maybe they dressed this way on purpose to get excused by the Fashion Police …

KATY PERRY CALLED. SHE WANTS HER HAIR BACK

What does your hair say about you?

Or, to be precise, what does your hair tell the *court* about you and your suitability as a juror?

Happily, there's a myriad of hairstyles you can adopt without having to resort to scissors or dyes. Even better, no one is going to be impolite and ask if you're wearing a wig or why your follicles are such a weird color that doesn't appear in the natural world. If what's on your head gives anyone cause to stare, it will very likely result in your being dismissed.

Let's start with your real hair first.

For women, ultra-short hair and wash-and-go bobs translate to individuals who don't want any fuss, bother or drama in their lives. They have places to go and things to do and being on jury duty for even a day just doesn't fit their agenda.

Men with very short hair (including buzz cuts) are likewise

perceived as wanting to spend as little time grooming as possible. It might also be assumed that they are ex-military, no-nonsense security guards or athletes who don't want their hair to, literally, weigh them down on the track or in the pool.

Redheads—both male and female—are perceived as fun-loving, easy-going and die-hard romantics that don't like to get bored.

High-maintenance hair that is gelled, moussed, sprayed and styled to have nary a single curl out of place denotes individuals of either sex who are fussy, self-critical and detail-oriented to the point of driving everyone around them crazy.

On women, bombshell blond hair is typically associated with sex appeal.

On men, it more likely conjures creepy reminiscence of *Harry Potter*'s Draco Malfoy and his dad, Lucius.

In contrast to French braids (which sometimes fall into the high-maintenance category of execution), mumsy braids or anything involving Scrunchies are popular with people-pleaser females who are used to putting the needs of everyone else before their own.

High ponytails on women are a sign of light-hearted fun. A

low ponytail on a man reflects a rebel who'd rather let his long hair flow free but is making a concession in order to conform to society.

Hair pulled back into a tight bun at the base of the neck or back of the head speaks to rigidity, strictness and inflexibility. And "man-buns?" Oh please, don't even get us started on how doofy they look.

Is your hair parted on the left, on the right, in the middle or not at all?

Left-parters are fiercely driven, smart and goal-oriented.

Right-parters rely more on their hearts than their heads to make decisions.

Center-parters are conscientious, trustworthy and balanced.

Having no part at all is reflective of spontaneity ("I can go either way") and a refusal to play games or spread gossip.

MAKING A STATEMENT WITH COLOR

It used to be that if you saw someone with pink, purple or turquoise hair, you assumed they were wearing a wig. If their hair was greenish-yellow, it probably meant they had spent too much time in the swimming pool. If it was grey, wild and unkempt like Einstein, you guessed they had long ago lost their battle with the hairbrush and just let everything do what it wanted.

Nowadays, you just don't know. Costume wigs are relatively cheap and don't put your own hair at risk with chemicals and dyes. You can also opt for temporary colors in the form of mascaras, chalks and hairsprays. Nor do you have to do your entire head. Go for streaks, just roots or just tips. Keep in mind that unconventional colors suggest unconventional thinking.

- Pink hair denotes a rabid aversion to confrontation. It's sweet, feminine and touchy-feely.
- Purple hair is all about psychic connections, spiritualty and rebellion.
- Green hair conjures Earth Mothers who strive for healing, growth and natural balance.
- Blue hair suggests its wearer is calming and confident but can project aloofness as well.
- Yellow or orange can't help but draw comparisons to cartoons. Come on now, is anyone going to take you seriously? Maybe you really don't want them to.

- Black? If it's not your natural color and you are of a very pale complexion, a jet black, Gothic dye is all about being radical, creative and strong-willed.

THE SKUNK STRIPE

A bold white stripe down the middle of black hair is going to get attention and not necessarily favorable. Having half your hair black and the other half white works pretty well, too. Could anyone rock this look better than Cruella de Vil? The first impression is that you are someone who believes the best use of puppies is in fur coats. If you wore a jacket with a fur collar, it would only emphasize this.

THE WIDOW'S PEAK

Can anyone look at a widow's peak and not be reminded of Eddie Munster? Okay, there are plenty of celebrities that have this particular hairline—Fran Drescher, Jude Law, Annette Bening, Leonardo DiCaprio, Kourtney Kardashian, Keanu Reeves, Ali Landry, John Travolta, Keri Russell, Chris Noth—but this V-shaped point typically isn't the first thing you notice about them. Eddie Munster, though? If someone mentions his name, it's the first thing you remember about what he looked like.

An old wives' tale about widow's peaks had ties to the supernatural; specifically, if you were born with one, your future spouse would die young. If this is a spooky look you want to go for, there's no shortage of YouTube videos on how to craft one with a cheap wig and a pair of scissors.

PIGTAILS

Unless you're channeling Mary Ann from *Gilligan's Island* or the young miss who graces the label of Vermont Maid Syrup, pigtails just look juvenile on anyone over the age of nine.

THE SHAGGY DOG LOOK

If your bangs are so long that they are covering your eyes and you have to keep sweeping them aside, how keen an observer are you going to be of what's going on in the courtroom?

BAD HAIR DAY

Your coiffure doesn't have to look perfect when you go to court. In fact, the *less* perfect it looks, the better your chances of getting excused. Damp hair, wildly flyaway hair, knit or plastic headbands, hair bows or a dangling pink foam roller you "forgot" to remove are all signs of someone who just can't get it together.

LOST IN TRANSLATION

When jury notices are mailed out, the senders have no idea whether the recipients are fluent in the English language. While a lack of written and verbal fluency in English isn't an automatic disqualification from service, there's a good chance of being excused if one shows up and politely explains that English isn't his/her native language.

In some jurisdictions, the fluency question is listed upfront on the form or in the online registration. In other jurisdictions, the judge asks for a show of hands which, ironically, means that the prospective jurors understand *why* they are raising their hands.

In another bit of irony, many jury summons are now being printed in multiple languages so that recipients will know what it is they have just received and where/when they are expected to show up.

Understanding the Chinese or Persian translation on the notice, however, is no guarantee of being able to follow courtroom proceedings once they get there.

Both of my manicurists are Vietnamese. A pair of lovely

women who have been in the U.S. for over 20 years, are naturalized citizens and have raised their families here.

Nonetheless, a jury summons has a major disruptive impact on their workaday livelihood and the schedules of their devoted clients.

And so, despite the fact they can both carry on lively conversations with their customers in perfect English, they are not averse to playing the "So sorry but I am very confused" foreigner card when necessary to get out of something they really don't want to do.

This involves smiling a lot, nodding for no particular reason, making themselves look as tiny as possible, scrunching their foreheads as if trying to absorb what is being said, speaking extra slowly, asking—oh so very politely and quietly—for questions to be repeated, and deliberately using the wrong words in their replies.

They are unapologetic fashionistas and yet show up for jury duty in plain cotton t-shirts or light cardigans, straight skirts, no stockings and generic tennis shoes.

One of them has also found it effective to keep an

inexpensive little purse in her lap and to clutch the top of it tightly as if it contains her most valuable possessions.

Everyone loves them because they are obviously trying very hard to be an earnest part of the process. And every single time, they are thanked and excused.

HOW TO GET YOURSELF OUT OF JURY DUTY

CAN YOU HEAR ME NOW?

If you clip off the thin cable at the base of an ear bud, the latter is pretty much indistinguishable from a visible hearing aid.

The success of this creative wriggle is to be able to pretend that no one is paying any attention to what you're doing. Which, of course, they will *all* be doing after a relatively short time.

After a moment in the jury box, look frustrated and as if you're straining to hear.

Remove the ear bud, scowl at it and put it back in. After a few seconds, take it out, shake it, flick your index finger at it and put it back in. Take it out again, study it, blow on it and put it back in. Take it out, muse a moment and then put it into your other ear. Nope, that didn't work, either.

Repeat.

If the judge or the attorneys ask if there's a problem, reply that it's old or it's new "and just needs some time to heat up."

HOW TO GET YOURSELF OUT OF JURY DUTY

BRIGHT SHINY OBJECTS

Courtrooms are well lit places so everyone can see what's going on. Accordingly, those bright overhead lights will reflect off of any large, shiny jewelry. This is not unlike scenes in Westerns when someone way atop a hill pulls out a pocket mirror and uses the glare of the sun to let everyone in the distance know exactly where they are.

A shiny metal pendant, blingy earrings and sparkly cuff bracelets accomplish the same thing. Every time you move, that shimmery glimmer is going to be a distraction to anyone in your line of sight. While it's simple enough for a judge or counsel to ask you to please remove them while you're in the courtroom, it's nonetheless worth a try.

HOW TO GET YOURSELF OUT OF JURY DUTY

NOT WHAT IT'S CRACKED UP TO BE

Before you enter the courtroom, take a couple of squirts of a saline nose spray. This will cause you to visibly sniff and snorfle. If you combine this with nervous fidgeting, scratching and suspicious eye-darting, no one in their right mind will want you on the jury. For extra effect, go for a very light dab of red lipstick at the base of both nostrils.

In the event you get pulled aside and asked if you're "on" something, you can very innocently reply that you're getting over a killer cold and the acetaminophen is really messing with you. You can even show them the perfectly innocent nose spray itself.

Will they believe you? Of course not. Because these are exactly the kinds of sneaky things that crackheads will say and do to feign innocence.

HOW TO GET YOURSELF OUT OF JURY DUTY

JUST WANTING TO HELP, YOUR HONOR

Employ reverse psychology and project unabashed excitement about being in a real courtroom. Total coolness! This is even better than all the *NCIS, Law and Order*, and *CSI* episodes you binge-watched last week to properly prepare for jury duty. Express your interest in wanting to help out in any way that you can since you consider yourself somewhat of an expert on courtroom procedures and interrogation.

HOW TO GET YOURSELF OUT OF JURY DUTY

IRRITABLE BOWEL SYNDROME

When asked whether there is anything that might inhibit you from being a good juror, volunteer that you have recurrent constipation or diarrhea which requires you to go to the bathroom every 30 minutes or so and is everyone okay with that?

HOW TO GET YOURSELF OUT OF JURY DUTY

SWASH SWASH BUCKLE BUCKLE

Does anything project BadAss better than a black eyepatch? The very sight of one bespeaks Mystery, Danger and Risk-Taking, especially if it graces the face of someone impossibly good looking and immaculately dressed. The intrepid Brenda Starr (a comic pages heroine modeled after Rita Hayworth) had a steamy relationship for years with the eye-patched and charismatic scientist Basil St. John. Can you get any more roguish and swashbuckling than that? Give this man a pirate ship and he'd fit right in. Where he *wouldn't* fit in would be in a jury box with 11 other people who would constantly be stealing covert glances and wondering how he came to be missing an eyeball.

Did St. John ever get called for jury duty? Not that we can recall. If he did, though, he already had a built-in excuse. Without regular injections of black orchid serum, he would succumb to a rare and exotic disease for which there was no cure.

Seriously. You can't make this stuff up.

HOW TO GET YOURSELF OUT OF JURY DUTY

PLANETARY INTERFERENCE

When asked whether there is any reason you believe you could not serve successfully on a jury, reply in your most serious voice, "Mars is in conjunction with Jupiter this week and is affecting my ability to make rational decisions."

Heavy black eyeliner, intense eyeshadow, one hoop earring and crystals are a kooky touch as well.

HOW TO GET YOURSELF OUT OF JURY DUTY

CASTING CALL

I always feel sorry for anyone who has one of his/her legs in a cast. Having to keep a limb immobile for a couple of weeks during the healing process is a major inconvenience. How do you take a shower? How do you drive a car? How do you get in and out of a car as a passenger? How do you maneuver a tray of food in the cafeteria? How do you get anywhere with the same speed, grace and agility as people whose legs *aren't* in casts?

In the interests of wriggling out of jury duty, you don't even have to break anything to make for a sympathetic presence in the courtroom. Not only are there easy demos on YouTube about how to create a fake cast but you can also purchase knee brace immobilizers at Amazon, Target and Walgreens. You can even buy a pair of crutches to finish off the look.

When called to the jury box, take your time. Take a *lot* of time. Fumble with this navigation and allow one of the crutches to fall with a clatter. People in close proximity will immediately dive in to assist you. Apologize profusely for inconveniencing them, all the while maintaining a "brave" face. Oftentimes there will be two or three short steps up to the jury box. Oh dear! Even though the steps are short, someone is going to have to help you with this since you can't bend your knee. You'll also have to sit on the aisle because the space in front of you affords about as much room as a seat on Southwest.

All of this will leave two impressions. The first is that you really shouldn't be out and about and, instead, should be at home resting. The second is that your impairment—let's be honest—is going to be a nuisance and will likely hold things up. Since everyone else wants to spend as little time in the courtroom as possible, it would simply be easier to excuse you.

Cautionary note: What are you going to say if the judge or legal counsel should ask about your mishap? Best to have a story up your sleeve and preferably one which attests to a lack of common sense. If it's summer, for instance, you can say you fell off the roof taking down your Christmas lights.

Or that you fell off the toilet hanging a picture.

Or that your Bird scooter hit a pothole.

Or your karate instructor told you that you weren't quite

ready to break a board with your foot ... and you didn't listen.

Or that you and your partner were practicing the "Time of My Life" lift from *Dirty Dancing* and s/he fell on your leg.

INKLINGS

The type, size and placement of a tattoo can say a lot about the person sporting it. According to *Psychology Today*, it can project that the individual is an extrovert, a nonconformist and/or a sentimentalist who wants a pictorial remembrance of experiences, relationships or cultural connectivity they can carry around on their skin.

Tattooing dates back to Neolithic times and evolved into a nonverbal way of communicating social status, ritualistic rites of passage, punitive "branding" for offenses, and slave ownership. In the age of our cave ancestors, it might even have been a way to express, "If found, please return to_____." In modern times, tattoos reflect the pride of belonging to a unique "club," be it the United States Navy, an ethnic tribe such as the Maori, or a neighborhood gang.

Tattoos also bespeak undying affection and the assumption the lovebirds are destined for eternity. (Unlike when Johnny Depp broke up with girlfriend Winona Ryder and had *Winona Forever* edited to read *Wino Forever*.)

Whatever the motivation behind body art, courtrooms across the country make a clear case for not wanting prospective jurors' tattoos to be visible. Hence, long-sleeved shirts and long pants if your limbs are a Technicolor billboard. Obviously if you have a tiny butterfly on your ankle or the back of your hand, it's not going to be a big deal. A tattoo on your face and neck is a lot harder to hide (especially if it's not real to begin with).

A friend of my youngest daughter likes to wear a blouse with long sleeves that can easily be pushed up to the elbows once she's inside the courtroom. She then proceeds to give a casual stretch with fingers locked and her inner arms facing the legal counsel. It takes only a brief glimpse of her inner-arm purple snakes to make them decide she is one suspiciously scary chick.

PIERCINGS

There is a generation which still believes that if God wanted you to have holes in your ears (or any other part of your body), He would have put them there.

Pierced ears have become so commonplace, we don't give them a second thought, much less a second look. But what about the woman—or man—who has filled every free space of the crescent ear lobe with some sort of bling? Or the one with the pierced cartilage? Or ginormous holes the size of a dime?

Don't even get me started on nose piercings, tongue piercings, lip piercings or eyebrow piercings. Eeek! I personally can't stop staring and wondering what possessed him or her to mutilate themselves in that way. I even had a former hairdresser who sported a gold nose ring which reminded me of Ferdinand the bull. He also had a pair of small ivory tusks which, when inserted in his nostrils, made him look like a warthog.

I certainly wouldn't encourage anyone to rush out and get

pierced just to try to get out of jury duty, especially when you can easily buy fake expanders, plugs, claws, septums and magnetic nose studs to emulate a rebel persona who isn't going to play well with others. By the by, it's unlikely you'll be asked to remove them in order to serve on a jury.

Well, except maybe for ivory tusks.

It all gets down to whether you're going to be a distraction. And distractions of any variety won't be of help to either side.

RASH DECISIONS

If I'm riding on public transportation and the only empty seat is next to someone with a weird rash, my preference will be to stand rather than sit next to them and risk our bodies touching. S/he could be a perfectly lovely person on the inside but on the outside—what *is* that thing?

Is it some sort of birthmark?

An allergic reaction to kale?

A freaky skin disease? If it's the latter, is it highly contagious?

Imagine this person stepping into the jury box and potentially making everyone else feel squirmy. Little would they suspect that this creative faker simply applied a mixture of red grease paint and liquid latex—both of which are harmless, inexpensive and can be purchased online or at any theatrical supply shop.

HOW TO GET YOURSELF OUT OF JURY DUTY

A MOLE AMONGST US

A beauty mark is a sexy euphemism for a facial wart. When we hear the term "beauty mark," thoughts are conjured of Marilyn Monroe, Cindy Crawford, Angelina Jolie, Anne Francis and Elizabeth Taylor.

Say the word "wart," though, and the images that spring to mind are fairy tale crones, ogres and trolls that live under bridges. The bigger the wart, the badder the personality behind it.

And then there's the issue of placement. A pert wart at the corner of the mouth, the top of the cheekbone or the outer corner of an eyebrow is sexy. A wart in the center of the chin or at the end of one's nose make it impossible to look anywhere else.

The cheapest way to effect a wart is with a black eyebrow pencil. If you're a DIYer who wants something more complex, mix some cornstarch and water, pop it into the freezer, scoop out a wart-sized particle, and glue it onto your face. You can also buy fake warts online and at Walmart during Halloween.

Cautionary note: If you're inclined to perspire when you're nervous, your self-affixed warts might slide off your face.

HOW TO GET YOURSELF OUT OF JURY DUTY

WAKE ME WHEN IT'S OVER

There's a gentleman in our church who habitually falls asleep about 15 minutes into the service. It's not that he's bored with the sermon. He's just one of those people whose brain hits the snooze button whenever he's required to sit still for long periods of time on a hard bench in a room that is pleasantly warm. He archly maintains that although his eyes are tightly closed, he's listening to everything going on.

Suffice it to say, it's the snoring which gives him away … along with leaning into his spouse and contentedly resting his head on her shoulder.

There are a lot of reasons a person could experience zzzs at inappropriate times:

Narcolepsy – a neurological disorder which causes intermittent episodes of drowsiness and nodding off in the middle of the day. Although there are treatments which can manage this condition, there is no known cure. Maybe not even injections of black orchid serum. A doctor's note would be required to use this excuse.

HOW TO GET YOURSELF OUT OF JURY DUTY

Insomnia. If someone has trouble falling asleep and *staying* asleep at night, his/her body is going to have to make up for it during the daytime. Unlike narcolepsy, insomnia is frequently treated with psychotherapy, the reason being that insomnia is often a product of extreme stress and anxiety about major life issues. It can be triggered as well by medical problems such as chronic back pain, arthritis, gastrointestinal problems, sleep apnea and asthma. Alcohol, caffeine, heavy dinners and nicotine? They're factors, too, along with an uncomfortable mattress, a room that's too warm or too cold, or too much light.

Party Hardy. How responsive are you going to be in court if you were out imbibing and dancing until the wee hours of the morning? Plus, you're going to have the haggard, disoriented look of someone with a hangover. It definitely will not inspire confidence.

Clocking In. Our circadian rhythms as human beings determine whether we're predisposed to be night owls or early birds. Night owls have no problem binge-watching episodes of *Game of Thrones* or Turner Classic Movies until 3 in the morning. Trying to roust them out of bed before noon, however, is not unlike poking a bear that's trying to hibernate. Trying to get them to the courthouse by 8am and then stay there until 4 is not a pretty sight.

Night Shift. There's a whole 'nother world going on long after the rest of us have hunkered down for the evening. It's happening in 24-hour eateries, factories, hospitals, law enforcement, hotels, security services and gas station mini-marts, just to name a few. If your job requires you to work the night shift, the only chance you have to sleep is during the day. This could actually qualify as a legal wriggle because your employer expects you to be operating on full thrusters when you show up at day's end.

If you're going to embrace a fake sleepyhead persona, the time to start it is when you're sitting in the courtroom but have not yet been called to the jury box. Park yourself near the front where you'll be more easily in the judge and the bailiff's line of sight. Yawn a lot. Fold your arms and allow your head to droop. If you *do* fall asleep, you'll be subject to jerky twitches and head-snaps (which are certain to gain notice). Squirm a bit in your seat as if you're really, really going to try to focus and stay awake.

Until you don't.

If/when your name is called, don't respond until the second or third time. Look embarrassed about dozing off. Insist that you can listen perfectly well with your eyes closed.

A WHISPER ON THE WIND

Don't you just hate it when you have to ask people to keep repeating what they've said because you couldn't hear them? There's nothing wrong with being soft-spoken but it drives court reporters crazy. If it's reflective of being really shy or really nervous, the court can't hold it against you. When your second and third attempts at cranking up the decibels *still* cause everyone to strain, it's going to make for a very long day to record your answers.

WORDSMITHING ASPIRATIONS

If you mention you're an aspiring crime/mystery/romance novelist or a coffeehouse poet, your chances of a dismissal are pretty high. Creative types are likely to overthink all of the testimony and evidence they're exposed to.

Plus the fact they are probably constructing their next chapter or stanza while they're supposed to be actively listening.

HOW TO GET YOURSELF OUT OF JURY DUTY

THERE'S GOT TO BE A MORNING AFTER

Whatever you're planning to wear for your first courthouse appearance, sleep in it the night before (especially if it's linen). Don't take a shower. Substitute a swig of rum for mouthwash.

HOW TO GET YOURSELF OUT OF JURY DUTY

SCENT OF A JUROR

Years ago I worked with a middle-aged guy who had convinced himself that patchouli cologne was a babe magnet. I don't know how many bottles Hank went through in any given month but he would liberally douse himself with the stuff every morning before he came to work. Not only could you always tell when Hank was in the building but also which elevators he rode and whether he went to the cafeteria. If you sat in a conference room for more than 20 minutes, you would start to feel faintly nauseous. Even two weeks later, the upholstery, curtains and carpeting reeked of this overpowering essence.

Some people's noses are way more sensitive than others. If you're lucky enough to be sitting in close proximity to one of them, they will probably not be shy in bringing it to someone's attention and singling you out for nausea-inducing olfactory assault.

HOW TO GET YOURSELF OUT OF JURY DUTY

DRESSING IN THE DARK

Wearing your clothes inside-out is a pretty good tip-off that you don't completely have it together.

ASKING STUPID QUESTIONS

Last but not least is the strategy of asking innocently inane questions. Among our favorites:

"Which one is the bad guy?"

"Is the cafeteria vegan?"

"Can we ask the suspect our own questions?"

"Do we get paid more if we take longer to make a decision?"

"When we do the voting thingy, will our ballots be secret?"

"Will this be on television?"

"I know we're not supposed to talk to anyone about the case, but can I tell my dog?"

"What happens to the attorney who loses?"

"Can I put jury duty on my resume?"

"Can we vote for the death penalty?" (especially amusing if it's a civil case)

HOW TO GET YOURSELF OUT OF JURY DUTY

ABOUT THE AUTHOR

Jan Miller is a humor writer who resides in Southern California.

HOW TO GET YOURSELF OUT OF JURY DUTY

HOW TO GET YOURSELF OUT OF JURY DUTY

FOR YOUR CONSIDERATION

"Family love," wrote Friedrich Nietzche, "is messy, clinging, and of an annoying and repetitive pattern ... like bad wallpaper."

A collection of mirthful essays about those who have never left, those who have left and come back (with extra baggage), and those who see Home as a revolving door through which to pass for free meals, laundry service and recharging batteries on a perpetual quest to find the meaning of life.

Available on Amazon in paperback as well as Kindle, Barnes and Noble, Apple, Kobo, Scribd, Tolino and Baker & Taylor

Excerpt from *Empty Nesters*:

"Just One More Thing ..."

Imagine, if you will, that Lt. Columbo's wife sends him to Bed, Bath & Beyond to buy a pair of holiday themed hand towels for the guest bathroom. A simple enough task, she thinks. She has even told him what aisle they're on so he can get in, get out and get home in time for lunch.

Almost four hours later, he still hasn't returned. Her first thought is that maybe there has been a murder in the cosmetics section and her beloved is busily jotting down witness statements in the tattered notebook he has pulled from the pocket of his rumpled raincoat.

"For all the time he spends at that job of his," her mother tells her, "you may as well have married a doctor." True enough, Mrs. Columbo thinks. But she also knows that LAPD's Homicide Department couldn't solve half their cases without her socially inept spouse's keen eye for detail.

In fact, he's using that keen eye right now with one of BB&B's clerks. "You know, sir, it's a funny thing. All my life I kept running into smart people. I don't just mean smart like yourself and the people in this fine store. You know what I mean. In school, there were lots of smarter kids. And when I first joined the force, sir, they had some very clever people there. But the thing I can't figure out—and stop me if I'm wrong—is that I haven't been able to find those little yellow pellets you put in the garbage disposal to make it smell nice. You know the ones I mean, right?"

Although the dishwasher pellets clearly weren't on the wife's list, neither was the set of Calphalon frying pans, chew-toys for the dog, a new doormat, his and her bedside reading lamps, a shower caddy, Hawaiian picnic plates, an electric toothbrush, an aqua laser steam mop, and 48 oz. of citrus shampoo.

By the time he pulls into the garage, every square inch of the Peugeot's trunk and passenger seat is occupied by a bulging white and blue bag. "You wouldn't believe the stuff they've got there," he tells his wife. She's pretty sure that even on his way out the door, he remembered one more thing he forgot to ask about.

"Did you remember the hand towels?" she asks him.

With the free hand that's not holding a cigar, he smacks himself in the forehead. "How could I have missed something so simple!" he declares. "I'll be right back …"

Gosh, but who does this fictional detective remind me of?

Unlike a lot of men who hate the idea of shopping and will spend as little effort as possible on it, the hubs will join me at the drop of a hat. If he answers to a siren's song, its name is Cost Plus World Imports.

We went there last weekend with a very short list in hand. That list contained olive oil, port, two bars of soap, chocolate and Italian hot sauce.

"We should check out the furniture as long as we're here," he says.

Over the years, we've bought a number of rustic and artsy-distinctive tables, credenzas, bookcases, curio cabinets with tile inlays, barstools and decorative mirrors that all look as if they carry an intriguing backstory involving smugglers in Borneo or casbahs in Morocco. There's even an 8' wooden giraffe, a bejeweled hookah and a hammered tin elephant in our family room. Why? Well, just because. He must have gotten out of the house that day when I wasn't looking and come home with items that serve absolutely no useful purpose.

He has laser-beamed in on a gorgeous storage cabinet with glass doors and formidable metal latches. Okay, to be honest, I think it's rather striking, too.

"We could really use one of these," he tells me.

"And where would it live?" I counter.

He shrugs. "I could find a place for it in my room."

This is a long-running joke between us. Whenever we buy something we don't really have a place for, it ends up in the hubs' home office and he's happy to accommodate it.

I recommend that we hold off for a while on this, my thinking being that if it's still there the next time we come back, maybe it's all meant to be. I'm also hoping that if we can just offload some of the people living with us, we'd have way more room to replace them with new furniture.

He's now saying we should see if there's anything new in plates.

I remind him that we have plates up the wazoo and are currently on a moratorium against buying any more. Not only do we have two tiers and three levels deep in our kitchen island but we also have plates stacked in almost every cupboard, the dining room hutch and the hall linen closet.

He asserts that one can never have *too* many plates and uses our own crowded household as a prime example. "What if we have company?"

Frankly, we could invite the entire student body, faculty and staff of Flintridge Prep to a five-course dinner and never run out of dishes to serve food on.

He picks up a turquoise dinner plate. "We don't have anything in *this* color," he says.

"We don't have anything in pink, either, but it's not a compelling reason to start a new trend."

"How about these placemats?"

"I don't think so."

"You know these napkin rings would really go with—"

"Nope."

"These martini glasses are interesting."

I shake my head.

To assuage his disappointment, I let him go hog-wild in the spice, condiments and sauces section. He even pounces on a package of novelty pasta wherein the noodles are shaped like the Space Needle. Because, hey, you never know when it's going to be exactly what you needed and you passed up the chance.

As the checker is ringing up our purchases, I realize we forgot to buy the bars of soap.

"I'm on it!" the hubs volunteers and eagerly skaddles off to the bath and body section.

I offer the checker an apologetic smile.

"We may be here for a while …"

www.ingramcontent.com/pod-product-compliance
Lightning Source LLC
Chambersburg PA
CBHW021434210526
45463CB00002B/506